ONE DAY CALLIGRAPHY MASTERY

The Complete Beginner's Guide to Learning Calligraphy in Under 1 Day!

Included: Step by Step Projects That Inspire You

By Ellen Warren

2

Calligraphy is one of the most fluid forms of art today. Typographers and iconographers as well as calligraphers use letters as a way of driving a point home more than just through the word itself, but through the way the word impacts you. Once you start looking at the way that words are made up, you'll begin to see the many ways that you can change them to have a bigger effect on the viewer. This is true of everything from invitations you send out to art you create for display. Words have specific meanings, but the way that a word is viewed versus heard can affect how it's perceived.

Calligraphy allows you to subtly enhance each letter, putting in different flourishes, curls, and lines. You can even add small pictures inside the words or letters to make each one a true type of art. Even when you perfect your calligraphy, it's still very difficult to get all your letters to look exactly the same each and every time. Small differences work their way in, which is part of what makes the finished effect so beautiful. To get the same effect out of a font, you'd have to go into each letter and warp it slightly, and even then you wouldn't quite achieve the beauty that comes from working with your hands.

Of all the art forms that I've studied and used over the years, calligraphy is one of the most underappreciated. After all, in an age of computers it's easy to add any type of script or font to just about anything. You can even purchase stencils and stickers in a variety of fonts as well if you want to add things to physical media.

I started learning calligraphy as a way to enhance certain pieces of art. It actually started when I began twisting wire into words. From there, I wanted to use some of the same words on wood and canvas to complete a set. But how could I get the same effect as I was getting from the wire? I needed a way to make the words decorative, even though what I was placing them on was not.

As I began looking at different fonts to reproduce, I realized that was I was looking for was calligraphy. A beautiful, elegant way to express letters and words by hand on any media from cardstock to wood. It didn't take me long to realize that calligraphy allowed me to personalize things far more than using a computer font or a sticker ever could.

I don't use calligraphy as frequently as I did when I first

discovered it, but I do use it to enhance specific pieces from time to time. Just knowing that it's available as a way to express myself, whether adding some text to a portrait or filling in an image with different words lets me be freer in my expression.

I've come to enjoy adding small flourishes to other pieces of art through the use of calligraphy. Whether I'm decorating the kitchen chalkboard for a new season or putting up a sign for the children's artwork I'm displaying, it's so easy to enhance your words through the use of calligraphy. I hope that you find similar uses for this art form once you begin as well.

Thanks!

Ellen Warren

Chapter Index

Introduction

Calligraphy is a visual art form, but one that varies tremendously from other art forms in that it has a long history of practical use. In addition, calligraphy can transcend the fact of its art and its creation to take on new meaning and to imbue additional meaning to the works that it's used to create. Many people simply view it as a method of writing, but calligraphy is really so much more. It's a means of perfecting your writing so that each letter transcends the word and becomes a piece of art all its own. At the same time, calligraphy is used to make each word into a work of art that amplifies its meaning.

This is what makes calligraphy have such an amazing impact on the viewer; you're not just looking at the word, you're taking in what the word brings with it whether flourish, form, art, or color. Think of a signature, and how people who sign things regularly will adapt a specific style. This is because they know that style helps impact the way that their signature is perceived – calligraphy does the same thing. A document written in calligraphy will be viewed very differently than a document saying the same thing but printed or using a plain text. This is why calligraphy is used to so frequently for important documents like diplomas, wedding invitations, and signs. When someone views a document written in calligraphy, it takes on more weight and a greater meaning than it had before on its own.

Unlike other forms of art, calligraphy truly needs to be mastered before you can really begin to explore it. There isn't a lot of personal interpretation in calligraphy; each letter still needs to have its original meaning, and to be at least somewhat recognizable. That's why calligraphy can be so intimidating for people to learn. Other art forms allow you to explore the medium while you perfect technique, but calligraphy demands perfection in each stroke. A person learning calligraphy may need to make the same letter in the same way again and again, much like a young child learning how to write for the first time. It's not uncommon to spend hours simply writing the same letter over and over, filling multiple sheets of paper until you feel so comfortable with it, that you can create it without thinking.

Once the basic forms of the letters you're mastering begin to become second nature, you can begin to put in the variations and flourishes that truly set calligraphy apart from simply a means of writing. You can also begin to explore different materials, such as embossing inks, paintbrushes, and split-tipped pens that will give your work variation and depth.

There are hundreds of different calligraphic fonts out there to explore. Some are fairly simple and are merely a slightly dressier way of writing. Others are extremely complex, with each letter having multiple flourishes that help give it greater impact. Because of this, it's not uncommon for a calligrapher to master two or three different styles. It's also common for beginners to start with a very basic script, then to begin working on different letter forms once the first set has been mastered. Whether you choose to stick with the first basic form, or you choose to master and use other forms later on is entirely up to you. It is recommended, however, that everyone begin with something simple so that you can learn how upstrokes vary from down strokes, and how to hold the pen and how much pressure to apply. All of this is much easier to learn on a simple script than on a more complex one. After you've gotten used to the materials and the methods, it's easy to transfer them to other forms.

This book is meant to help you learn the basics of calligraphy. You'll discover how material can change the look of a letter such as pen and ink versus a paintbrush, the best way to produce a stroke, and how to create your own personal expression. Like other art forms, a lot of calligraphy will take on your own personal style. Even copying a set of fonts will still let you introduce your own personality through the boldness of your stroke or the flourish of your ends. No two people will ever have quite the same writing style, even when using the same type of calligraphy or script simply accounting for the amount of pressure and the dexterity of your hand.

During this book you'll learn about the different styles of calligraphy, and how you go about learning a specific style. While not every style is listed here, the basic method of drawing each letter remains the same; once you've learned one style it's easy to adjust and move on to other styles and methods over time. Calligraphy fonts can be found everywhere, from books to invitations and greeting cards. If you find a style that calls to you, you'll be able to adapt and copy it by the time you've finished practicing the letters given in this book.

Towards the end of the book and after you've had a chance to practice forming letters, you'll find a few simple projects you can practice your calligraphy on. After all, it can get a little boring and repetitive to simply make the same letters again and again; it's a lot more fun to practice your letters on something that you can use, display, or give to someone else. Each project is completely customizable, from the size of the paper to what it is you decide to write, and even the style of calligraphy that you use. Once you've completed them, you may find that you'll want to explore different phrases and lettering of your own until you've gotten the hang of it. You may even want to make multiples of each one, using a different medium, background, and phrase each time until you truly feel that you've mastered each one. This can be a fun way to explore what a felt-tipped pen will do to your letters or to begin using a brush for the first time. After all, by making multiples of the same thing using different media, you can compare your end results easier and decide which method appeals to you the most.

By the time you've finished the book, you should have

a good understanding of what calligraphy is, and how you can apply it to your own art. You'll hopefully also see that while calligraphy can appear to be intimidating with its elegance and beauty that it's still an art from like any other that can be mastered through patience and time. In fact, unlike certain types of art where you need to develop an eye for color, space, and arrangement, nearly anyone can learn calligraphy in their spare time, regardless of what other artistic talents you may or may not posses.

Brief History of Calligraphy

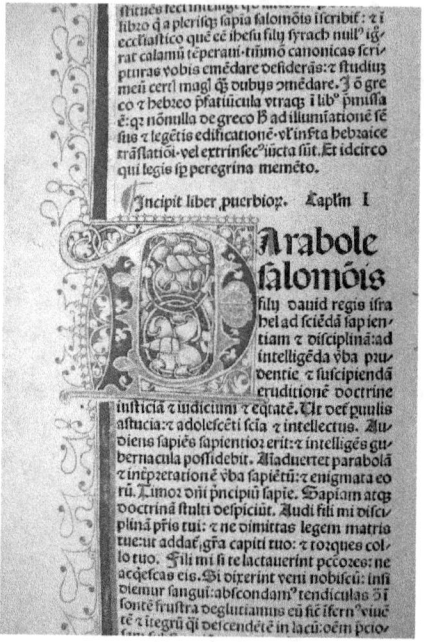

Traditional forms of calligraphy can be traced back to the Roman alphabet and some of the very first forms of writing that there were. The letters that are still found carved into stone and painted on walls evolved slowly over a few centuries to begin to be recognizable as the script that is still used today.

They began as capital letters, followed by the introduction of lowercase letters, before they then gradually evolved into script, and finally into the Roman alphabet, with the specific lines and flourishes that are still recognizable today.

Eventually, as literacy began to spread throughout Europe, books and bibles began to be hand lettered, using one of a few different uncial scripts. These further evolved as more letters and words needed to be fit onto a page, with the Gothic script becoming the preferred method because of the size of the letters and the ease with which they could be recognized. Gothic script remained one of the most popular forms of calligraphy until the printing press was invented, and even then some of the first books printed still used the Gothic style.

Most hand-lettered books were considered a work of art by themselves. They needed to be not only legible, but uniform, and they were often accompanied by illustrations to enhance the text. Only those who were truly proficient in calligraphy were commissioned to produce these books, which is how the art form began to emerge. A true calligrapher could spend years creating one book, developing his own style of writing that was complemented by the borders, colors, and illustrations on each page. Books were treasured during this time, simply for the amount of time and care that went into each one.

Calligraphy in Use Today

Interestingly, it was the invention of the printing press that truly launched calligraphy as an art form that is still in use today. While each calligrapher had his own style, most used a very basic set of letters, and few really experimented with changing them once a script began to be an accepted version. Once the printing press began to be widely spread, however, it opened the door to distinction. Different typesetters began to create their own fonts, with artists beginning to design fonts that were easier to read and could fit more words onto a page. Eventually, with the invention of computers more decorative fonts needed to be created to personalize and decorate a wide variety of different items from signs to websites. It is still common for iconographers today to create specific fonts for books and other means of printing to help enhance the look and style of a page.

Calligraphy today has taken on a life of its own separate from the fonts and lettering that first launched it. Now letters can be formed in any shape, including those that are unintelligible or unreadable. Iconographers, or people whose job it is to create new letters and fonts, may sometimes make their letters into true pieces of art that have little to do with the alphabet. Think of the "ding bats" that you can translate your text into simply highlighting a word and changing the font in a computer program.

Because of this, calligraphy can be said to be either traditional, or stemming from the Roman alphabet that spawned the art form, or non-traditional and letters that are completely different and are an art form all their own.

Calligraphy is most often seen today on things like wedding invitations and logos, but it can also the basis for new types of fonts, as well as any type of lettering from banners and signs to greeting cards. Typographers whose job it is to create new kinds of type and fonts may use calligraphy as the base of their work. They may also use a variety of calligraphy types including traditional and non-traditional letters, with many typographers mastering both forms.

Anyone that needs to add letters to anything from art to signs can use calligraphy as the base of their work. Calligraphy styles have evolved so much that there are countless fonts in use today, from the very simple to the extremely complex.

Beginning calligraphers may want to work on mastering at least two styles to start with, one in the traditional sense and one non-traditional. This can help you develop a base to begin creating your own personal style.

Styles of Calligraphy

There are countless different calligraphy styles, with more being created every day. Broadly, however, they can be broken down into two categories: traditional and non-traditional.

Traditional letters are those that are directly derived from the Roman alphabet. This includes the Gothic style, such as this letter A:

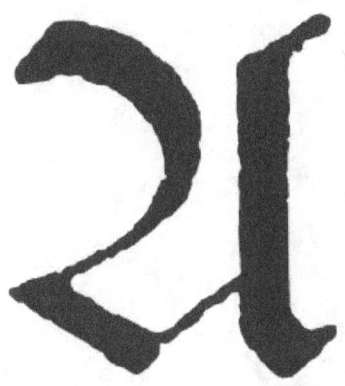

Traditional letters can also be simple scripts or handwritten letters, like this classic A:

Traditional letters can also be extremely ornate. The basic form of the letter remains the same; it's the flourishes the surround the letter that begin to set it apart as a form of art, like this ornate A:

Non-traditional letters can begin to incorporate different types of lines. The letters themselves may still be recognizable, like this formal A:

They may also start to include additional lines, which can help add dimension to the letters, like this "Adorable" A:

Non-traditional letters can take on a number of different personas, however. This is where art truly comes into play along with calligraphy. While traditional letters may be plain or ornate, they are still generally recognizable at all times. Non-traditional letters, however, may include a variety of other images, or they may be completely unrecognizable as the letter they are conveying. Non-traditional letters are some of the most fun to learn, and the most fun to start including in different projects. Because they can often take on the look of something else entirely, they can be used to help bring greater impact to the word they are describing. This letter A, known as a BreastBomb, is a good example of how a letter may start to become something else:

When paired with other letters, you may be able to make out the word. On its own, however, this A could simply be an abstract form of art. With the shape of the letter calling to mind a sailboat or even a shark fin, think of how this style of letters could be used to create a sign or logo for a boat business or a bait shop. This is where calligraphy can become more art than script, and yet retain its original purposes.

How Materials Affect Style

Traditionally, calligraphy is produced using a pen and ink. Things have changed, however, with the introduction of non-traditional letters and letter forms. In addition, while original calligraphers may have only had access to a pen and ink, today people have access to countless types of pens, markers, brushes, and other media that can be used to distribute ink on a page. Brushes, ball-point pens, and felt-tipped pens can all be used in calligraphy today to produce a variety of different looks. The same letter, drawn the same way but using a different material can produce a very different look.

This is due in part to how thick the ink is applied to the page. A felt-tipped pen is going to deliver far more ink in a single stroke than a traditional pen tip will. On the other hand, it's a lot more difficult to get an angle out of a thick, felt-tip than you can out of something thinner. It's also easier to put pressure on a felt-tipped pen, so while with a traditional pen you could easily lift it from the page to lighten your stroke or even take a break in mid letter, you may have a harder time doing this with a felt-tipped pen, which will render your letters in a different way.

Brushes can add a lot of texture to your letters, depending on the size of brush that you use. For example, a thin brush will often get you similar results to a pen, while a thicker brush may distribute the ink unevenly, giving you lighter and darker areas. Likewise, any brush has the ability to thin out the ink at the end of a stroke. This may allow some of the individual brush fibers to separate, making additional marks on the page. And while it's easier to get the lighter upstrokes using a traditional pen than a felt-tipped one, it's a lot harder to get the darker down strokes from a brush. You simply don't have the leverage necessary to lean on the brush hard enough to get the dark down stroke without also spreading out your brush and producing a wider, less defined mark.

Some types of calligraphy need the kind of separation that a brush can make to help produce a texture to the letter. For example, this Jellyka Castles A is much easier to produce with a brush that has had its fibers separated, than with a pen or a marker:

On the other hand, a similar effect can be achieved with a very fine-tipped pen that is scratched over and over again through the surface of the letter. In many cases, the choice of material that you use will be dictated largely by personal taste.

Using Brushes

Brushes are more difficult to control because you don't press them on the paper for each part of the stroke. As mentioned previously, they also have a tendency to distribute their ink more unevenly than a pen may. However, brushes come in so many different sizes that you can often get better results by using a brush to produce much larger letters such as those that may be placed on a sign or canvas.

Alternatively, if using brushes for larger works where

you want to gain a lot more control, you may wish to outline your letters using pen and fill them in using the brush afterward. Brushes add a layer of unpredictability to any project, which can be fun depending on the type of letter that you're trying to produce.

For very ornate and formal letters, however, you may want to stick to using a pen simply for the level of control it gives you. While this can limit the size of the project, it will still help you get the results you're looking for.

Using Pens

While brushes come in a variety of different sizes, pens come in a variety of different types of tips. Some tips will deliver the ink to the page at a very constant rate, which can help you gain more control over your project. Others will require you to maintain a more even touch of pen to paper the entire time to avoid accidentally delivering more ink in some areas. Even the shape of the pen itself can have an impact on your work. Straight pens can be a lot easier for a beginner to hold than curved pens, for example. Once you've perfected your letters on one pen, you may want to try switching anything from the nib to the pen itself to see how it affects your work.

26

When you begin, you may want to try a few different types of pens as you practice. This is because you will get very different results. In some cases, you may find that simply practicing with a specific pen over and over again will get you more consistent results that will help you achieve the look you want. In other cases, however, you may also find that an inconsistent result can be pleasing to the eye and can help you achieve a different type of letter than you may have originally been trying for. As with any art form, calligraphy is a mixture of mastery and expression; don't be afraid to try using several different types of pens to produce a variety of results even if they don't look like you first intended.

Materials to Use as a Beginner

As previously mentioned, you'll probably want to try out a variety of different materials as you get started, until you find a few that you're comfortable with and that give you the kinds of strokes you're looking for. That said, you'll need to pay attention not only to the pens or brushes, but also to the type of material that you're working on.

Like many art forms, your media is made up of a few different parts. In this case, the ink, what you use to apply it, and what you apply it to. You have a lot of different choices for what you'll put your ink on, including:

- Cardboard
- Canvas
- Paper
- Wood
- Cardstock

As you begin practicing your strokes, however, you may want to invest in some heavy, watercolor paper.

Watercolor paper is made to absorb extra water from your brush or pen. This will help make sure that your strokes aren't too heavy at first, because any extra moisture will be pulled into the paper, rather than beading up off the surface. Watercolor paper is therefore a great medium for working with traditional pen-and-ink, as well as beginning to work with brushes.

It isn't the best paper, however, if you plan on working with either felt-tipped pens or with a ballpoint pen. Watercolor paper is heavily textured, which is what helps pull in the water. This means that it may pull extra color from a felt-tipped pen, so if you leave your pen in place just a little too long, the color will spread too quickly. Likewise, the texture of the paper may make it difficult to get a smooth stroke from a ballpoint pen.

For these two pens, you may want to look for some very smooth paper. Like the watercolor paper, you'll want to ensure that whichever one you choose is heavy or high in pounds. This will help ensure that your colors don't bleed, while the smooth surface will allow your pen to move cleanly across it.

Whichever paper you first begin using, take the time to

either print or draw some lines across it. Think of a kindergartener learning how to print. He'll use a lined sheet of paper so that he can ensure that each of his letters is the same height, and that they move neatly down the row together. Think of those lines like a guide; they will enable you to focus on the shape of the letter and not on its size or position on the page. Once you've gotten used to shaping your letters, then you can try working without the guides and focusing more on size and position.

Remember, too, that you'll want to adjust the size of your lines and of your letters according to the type of pen or ink you're using. For example, a very fine-tipped pen can produce small or elaborate letters with thin lines. A heavy brush or a felt-tipped pen, however, will require that the same letter be much bigger in order to accommodate the size of each stroke.

It's OK to play around with several sizes of pen or brush as you begin; you may find that you get a different effect from different sizes of the same pen or brush making the same letter. Once you've had some practice shaping your letters and determining what it is you want them to look like, you'll also have a good idea of which size and type of pen or brush to use to get those effects.

Keep in mind, however, that it can be very tempting to simply reach for what you're already familiar with, such as pencils, ballpoint pens, and felt-tipped markers. And while it is entirely possible to learn calligraphy using those materials, you won't get many of the same traditional looks and styles that you'll get from using a pen with a bottle of ink or even a brush. Part of learning any new art form is stretching yourself, so even if you like the look of heavy letters that can be achieved using a chiseled edge marker (one of my favorite mediums, in fact) you can still benefit from learning how to use more traditional materials at the same time.

That said, when getting started you'll probably want to invest in:

- A straight pen – this the part of the pen that you'll hold. Straight is much easier to get used to than something curved
- A nib designed for beginners, such as the Zebra G Nib
- Ink of your choice

To use the pen and ink, you'll push the nib into the pen base until it's secure. Then dip the tip of the nib up to the hole into the ink. When the hole is completely covered, "wipe" the nib against the bottle to remove excess ink. You'll now be able to begin practicing your letters. If you find that your pen is beginning to clog, a rag of some kind can be used to clean it as needed.

After you've started practicing, you can try not only a few different pens or nibs, but also some different papers. Cardstock often makes a nice choice, as it's smooth enough to give you a good result without bleeding the ink. Always pay attention to the weight of the paper to help avoid the ink blotting through.

Basic Calligraphy Strokes

A lot of learning calligraphy is going to be learning how to control your pen, and how to get the right amount of pressure on it to produce the kind of line you're looking for. So before you begin attempting to draw letters, you're going to want to spend some time getting used to your pen.

Start out with a sheet of watercolor paper, and draw or print a series of lines on it as if you were using paper to begin writing out the alphabet for the first time. Dip your pen in ink, and start practicing a short, downward stroke with the pen.

Don't press down on the pen as you draw; you want to simply let the ink flow from the nib. Once you've made a row of short downward strokes, begin a second row pressing down lightly on the pen. You'll notice that by pressing down slightly, your line will begin to thicken.

Spend the next row of lines you make on the paper experimenting with the thickness of your lines by varying the amount of strength you use to press down on the nib. You should notice a distinct difference in line, as well as occasional blots. The blots will occur if you leave your pen in any one spot for more than a second, so take care to lift your pen straight up off of the paper as soon as you complete each line. You may also want to practice stopping your line mid-stroke, then beginning it again. Some very ornate letters will require you to stop mid-letter, then begin again. Over time, this should become seamless, so you are unable to identify where you took your pen from the paper.

Once you've gotten the hang of creating a simple down stroke, begin practicing an upstroke. Rather than simply drawing a line from bottom to top, however, you'll want to begin making a simple loop that starts at the bottom, goes up, and continues down again. Think of it like a cursive, lowercase letter L.

Begin your loop on your practice line, moving up the paper and slightly to the right before curving to the left and returning down again. This will allow you practice not only the downward stroke you just learned, but an upward stroke and a curve at the same time. Repeat this for a row or two the same way you made your down strokes; varying the weight of the lines by giving more or less pressure to the nib.

Once you've gotten the hang of the lowercase L, move on to the other lowercase ascending letters. These are b, d, f, h, k, and t.

In calligraphy script, they'll look like this:

b d f h k t

Plan on spending a minimum of one page on each letter as you master the strokes. The key to forming your lowercase ascending letters is to go very light on your up strokes, but harder on the down stroke. This is what will give your letters some depth and dimension; each letter will have thinner lines where you stroke up, and heavier lines where you stroke down.

After you feel you've mastered the lowercase ascending letters, begin on the lowercase descending or g, j, p, q, and y.

Scripted, they'll look like this:

j p q y

Exactly like the ascending letters, you'll make each up stroke lighter than your down strokes. By now, you should start to see the reason behind this; your hand as you move downward on the paper is naturally going to become heavier, bearing down on the pen and producing a heavier mark. The key is going to be to regulate how hard you press down on each stroke; you'll want each letter to be uniform to the one next to it as you move across the page.

Finally, move on to the final lowercase letters – a, c, e, i, m, n, o, r, s, u, v, w, x, and z –

a c e i m n o r s u v w x z

The same rules apply to these letters as to the others. The difference is that these letters are more uniform in size, and don't have the larger swoops. After practicing the letters that ascend and descend so dramatically, these should come much easier. Once you've dedicated a page to each of these letters, move on to the uppercase calligraphy script alphabet:

A B C D E F
G H I J K L M
N O P Q R S T
U V W X Y Z

Once you've had a chance to practice both the uppercase and lowercase script alphabets (and don't worry if this takes you several days. It can be very relaxing, however, to simply write the same letter again and again. Just pick a time of day when you can clear your head and write out a page or two of letters.) it's time to begin working on joining them up into simple words. This is usually the tricky part, and the most intimidating. Writing a letter on its own, spaced apart from the rest allows you to see it as an individual. But when you join it up to others, it

39

becomes part of something bigger, and that something needs to be a little more uniform. This means that your letters are really going to have to be uniform in both size and weight. This isn't actually as hard as it sounds, but it does mean that you'll need a little bit more practice, this time on joining your letters, rather than forming them. This is where your lined paper will really come in handy; you'll want your letters to move evenly across the page, and as a beginner you may find that instead they invariably slope downhill until you learn to control your hand.

To start, focus on small, short words, such as if, it, is, or as. Then you can begin to move on to three letter words, the, cat, dog, big. The idea is to pay attention to how your letters connect – or don't connect. Remember, this is just one calligraphy alphabet and one style of writing. Some alphabets leave letters slightly apart from one another, so if you aren't invested in learning script, you can simply move on to another alphabet or make your own. Formal writing isn't actually the same as script, and many formal calligraphy types don't connect at all. The letters will still relate to one another, however, simply because of how close or far you'll need to place them. Whichever alphabet you begin to use, take the time to start spelling out simple words until you get a feel for how they interrelate.

if, it, is, as

the, cat, dog, big

Notice that even in script, not every letter joins the ones beside it. As the artist, you'll be able to make decisions regarding the placement of the letters, and how they relate to one another, as well as style of writing. Take time as you write out your simple words to play around with how they interact with one another. You may find that some words are easier to combine, or that some words have a bigger impact if some space is introduced into them.

Remember that writing words that are joined means that you'll need to pay closer attention to the amount of ink in your nib. While individual letters are easy to track the level of ink in, and to replenish as needed, it's a little harder when you're writing a larger word. This is where your practice of lifting the pen from the page is going to help pay off; you'll be able to stop and start a word if you begin to run out of ink without having to interrupt the flow of the writing.

After you've had time to practice shorter words, start writing longer ones or even sentences. At this point it really won't matter what you write; it's the practice that counts. You need to be able to write and join up your letters easily without having to stop and think about their shape or how they'll interact with those around them. So keep writing and practicing until each letter is second nature.

Tips for Beginning

A lot of what you'll be doing at this point is simply practicing the same letters and words over and over. These few tips can help you and prevent some common issues from cropping up;

- Don't scratch. If you hear your pen scratching against the paper it means that you're holding it incorrectly. Try adjusting your grip until you no longer hear it.
- Keep a wet towel handy. If your notice that your pen is beginning to clog up with dried ink or that it's beginning to leave some blobs behind, just wipe it on the towel.
- Pay attention to word spacing. Letter spacing is important, but so is word spacing. Try putting

just a little extra space between words in a sentence to give your words a bigger impact.

- You can lift your pen in the middle of a letter. It's OK to take your time and to take a break mid-letter or mid-word. Just lift your pen straight up to help prevent blots. No one will know that you took a break, but to help minimize small blots or errors, try lifting your pen on the down stroke, rather than the up while your line is heavier.

- Experiment with a variety of different papers and cardstocks. You want a nice, heavy weight that doesn't feather or bleed the ink as you write on it. Some stores have a practice sheet of paper set out for you to try, other papers will list calligraphy or pen and ink as one of their intended uses; these will probably serve you better in the long term.

Practice Projects

Practice, practice, practice is really what it takes to truly become good at calligraphy. Unfortunately for many people, all of that practice can quickly begin to feel a little tedious and dull after a while. And when this happens, you're more likely to quit before you ever end up mastering it.

That's why I like to make practice projects when I'm learning a new letter formation. It enables me to practice those letters, without going completely insane writing page after page of A's, B's, C's, etc. The best part about practice projects, is that you can usually use them after you're done. Whether you want to make greeting cards to give to friends and family, or you want to create a sign to hang on the wall of your home, it can feel really good to make something that has a purpose, while helping you strengthen your craft.

To that end, the following projects are designed to help you practice your letters using a variety of different materials and media. This will help you begin to resize your letters and to see what will happen if you switch from a pen to a paintbrush to a felt-tipped marker. Before you take on these projects, you should be fairly used to making your letters, whether you choose to use the calligraphy script shown here, or you're choosing a different style all your own.

You can adapt the words and phrasing on the projects to meet your needs, or practice them as is. Either way, they can be a great way for you to continue learning calligraphy, while also having a little fun creating some art. Feel free to size the projects to fit your needs; there's nothing wrong with going super big or shrinking things down a little to a more manageable size. It's tough to use lined paper to practice making letters of varying sizes, which is part of what makes these projects so great; they let you hone your skills in a variety of ways without confining you.

Greeting Card

Greeting cards are becoming a lot less common these days, especially as more people begin to communicate exclusively online. That's why it's so charming to receive a handmade card these days. And what better way to show off your newfound calligraphy skills than by making your own cards?

Remember, one of the ways that calligraphy is still really relevant today is in card making – invitations, thank you notes, greeting cards, all of these utilize calligraphy to send the message to the reader. This is especially true for cards that don't have a lot of other imagery going on.

So while it is entirely possible to create a set of greeting cards using rubber stamps and paper images, why not try your hand at creating a few really elegant cards with calligraphy instead? Because the way that the words are formed becomes the focus of the card, you don't need to have a lot of extraneous imagery. This is especially great for anyone that is unable or unwilling to do a lot of cutting, piecing, and drawing to create their card.

Best of all, this can be a great way for you to practice writing out some very simple words and messages without your practice grid. To make things more interesting, try writing out your message using a variety of different inks or by using felt-tipped pens rather than a traditional pen and ink to vary the way that the words come out.

What you'll need:

- Heavy cardstock
- Scissors or rotary cutter
- Ruler
- Butter knife
- Pencil
- Eraser
- Pen and ink or felt-tipped pen in your choice of color
- Sheet of blank paper

What you'll do:

1. Trim the cardstock down to the size you want your finished card to be.
2. Measure the card to find the exact center and lay your ruler along this line.
3. Take the back – non-serrated – edge of your butter knife and press it deeply into the card stock right next to the ruler. Drag it along the edge of the ruler pressing hard on the card. This will score the card and make it easier to fold over.
4. Fold your card along the line you just scored.
5. Take a look at the front of the card. You'll want to plan where you put your letters. Do you want them in a single row or in two rows? Right in the center of the card, or asymmetrical? You'll also have to determine how big you'll want your letters to be and how much you'll want them to fill the card.
6. Lightly sketch a line or lines onto the front of the card with your pencil where the words will be placed. This will help you keep your letters even and in a straight line; you'll erase the pencil marks once you've finished your calligraphy, so draw very lightly with the pencil.
7. Tuck a blank sheet of paper into the card between the two halves. This will ensure that if

your cardstock absorbs too much ink or bleeds through that it won't affect the interior back surface of the card where you'll write your message to the recipient. If the ink does bleed through the cardstock on the inside front of the card, don't worry; you can cover this by gluing a decorative sheet of paper to the inside of the card, hiding the ink and brightening up your card at the same time.

8. Plan out what you want your message on the front of the card will be. You'll want this to be fairly simple and straight to the point; you want the writing itself to be the focal point so don't get too involved with the message.

9. Draw out your letters on the front of the card using your penciled lines as a guide. If you want, you can try adding some extra flourishes to your capital letters by starting them slightly to the left of the word and beginning and ending each your lines with an extra curve.

10. Allow the ink to dry completely, blotting if necessary, then erase the pencil marks. If you plan on adding a calligraphic message to the interior of the card, repeat these steps on the inside. Otherwise, simply write out a message to the recipient.

Decorative Sign

Decorative signs for your home's interior featuring a personal saying or a relevant quote are extremely popular right now. Some of them are printed on paper and framed, while others are painted onto larger boards or pieces of wood and hung as is for a rawer look. Either way, it can sometimes be difficult to find the perfect message or quote readymade to complement your home. By practicing your calligraphy, you can create your own personalized, decorative sign for any room of your home.

You are completely able to personalize this project from the saying itself to what you end up putting it on until you get the perfect accent piece for your home. I like the idea of using mildly decorative paper or paper with a printed border on it, then framing it, but you can use a piece of very smooth birch plywood, or even an old fence piece or pallet. Keep in mind that the rougher the material that you're working on, the smoother your writing implement. For example, while you may want to use a felt-tipped pen or pen and ink on canvas or paper to be framed, for writing on wood you'll need to try your hand at using a brush. Very smooth wood, like birch plywood, can generally handle the same ink you use on paper with little difficulty. Rougher woods, however, are likely to allow the ink to run and bleed a little, which can detract from your finished piece. In these cases, you'll want to use a thicker paint like acrylic to apply your words. The same rules apply when using a brush and paint as they do a pen and ink, but you'll find that you need to use a little more pressure on the brush throughout each letter to get the paint to transfer well. You may also want to break each letter into two or three pieces, and paint them individually, lifting your brush at the end of each stroke to apply more paint. This will give your letters the most consistent look.

Because printed signs are so popular right now, you may want to consider making a few using different materials until you feel comfortable with each one. Who knows? You may find that you're happier using brushes and paint than a pen and ink and revolutionize your whole art form.

What you'll need:

- Writing surface – canvas or watercolor paper, or wood
- Writing implement and media – pen and ink, felt-tipped pen, or brush and acrylic paint
- Pencil
- Ruler
- Eraser

What you'll do:

1. Plan what you'll write. Ideally, you want the saying or quote to completely fill the page or board. You can combine a few different calligraphy styles, stacking and arranging words if you like, or just spread them out evenly across the area.
2. Make sure that if you are using a board, that it's clean, dry, and smooth. If necessary, you may want to give it a base coat of paint to even out the surface before you write on it.

3. Plan where you will be placing your words and lightly sketch a line or lines onto the surface with a pencil to act as a guide for your lettering. Be sure to sketch as lightly as possible so that you can erase this line once you're done.

4. Begin writing. If you are switching to a brush or felt-tipped pen for the first time, you may want to practice on a piece of scrap paper or wood first. The heavier you press with the brush, the cleaner your lines will be; using the brush with a lighter touch may result in a feathering around the edges. You can always adjust your brush size and the amount of ink or paint on it as you go until you get the desired results.

5. Allow your ink or paint to dry completely, then erase the pencil marks to display.

Party Décor

Themed parties are all the rage right now, complete with signs directing guests, labels for the food you're serving, and decorative elements that can help the theme come together. Because many of these parties are fairly custom, it can be hard to find all the signs, labels, and decorations that you need at the store. With your new calligraphy skills, however, you won't need to worry; you can create your own labels and decorations in minutes. The best part about this is that you can also customize the color of ink you use, as well as the style of the writing.

For example, if you were having a beach-themed party,

you could use a calligraphy font that looked more casual or like ocean waves to help complete the theme. You can also use a wide variety of different scrapbook papers or cardstocks for the background to help further customize the look. In the above example, you could find some paper printed with palm trees or with a sand background to write on, really dressing up your party décor and giving everything a professional look.

This is where having the ability to do calligraphy can really come in handy. Whether you're planning a big party or a small holiday get together for family, being able to use calligraphy to dress up everything from décor to place cards can give your home or event the kind of special, polished treatment and look that will impress everyone that sees it. Best of all, you can create these professional looking details for a fraction of the cost of what it would be to purchase them readymade – and often times they come out even better looking as well!

What'll you'll need:

- Cardstock or paper in your choice of color or print
- Scissors or rotary cutter

- Butter knife
- Pen and ink or felt-tipped pen
- Pencil
- Ruler

What you'll do:

1. Cut or arrange your cardstock or paper to the correct size. If you're making labels for food or placements, consider folding your cardstock or paper so that they can stand up themselves on the table. To do this, find the center of the paper or card and place a ruler across it horizontally. Place the blunt side of the butter knife on the paper next to the ruler and press hard on the knife as you pull it across the paper several times to score it. Fold the paper along the line.

2. Locate where on the paper or cardstock you plan on writing your words or message. Lightly draw a pencil line or lines where the words will go so that you can keep your words even and centered on the page. Be sure to keep your pencil marks light as you will erase them once you are done.

3. Write your words or message on the paper or cardstock using a calligraphy style that complements your theme.

4. Allow the ink to dry completely, then erase the pencil marks from the card.
5. Display your labels, signs or décor.

Conclusion

Calligraphy is one of the oldest writing styles around. And yet at the same time, it's one of the most constantly changing and innovative art forms in use today. Iconographers and calligraphers are constantly working to create new fonts, new letters, and new ways of creating words as art. Some are meant to be purely decorative, but others are designed to bring a bigger impact to whatever it is that you're trying to say.

There's a reason why people often move to capital letters or bold fonts when trying to get a point across. Sometimes the visual impact of a word helps your understanding of its meaning. That's what calligraphy can do for a lot of different projects; it can enhance the impact of your words. Whether you're just looking for a more elegant way of expressing yourself, or you're looking to change the way that people view words, calligraphy can be a great way to impress a new meaning on to everyone that sees what it is you want to say.

While this book is aimed at beginners, and focuses on a

single font to begin with, you can use the exact same methods, tips, tricks, and techniques to learn any calligraphy style or to create your own. There are hundreds of different letter styles available today. Some have been created for single or artistic uses, such as letters formed out of flowers to spell out the words Spring, Nature, or Flower for an ad. Others have evolved to become variations on a single theme meant to enhance things like invitations and thank you cards. If you spend enough time looking at various fonts, you'll notice that they often have a similar base and that the slant of the letters or the amount of flourishes they contain is what sets them apart from one another. Therefore learning a single calligraphy style can allow you to branch out into multiple directions simply varying the base of the letter slightly.

Calligraphy is not meant to be a fast art form, nor is it something that you'll become proficient at overnight. It can take hours, days, and weeks of steady work and practice to achieve consistency between your letters in just one basic style. There is a beauty and a sense of peace in this practice, however, which can leave you feeling relaxed and introspective as you learn to form your letters.

Calligraphy is the perfect art form to learn on solitary

evenings or long days with no plans where you begin to itch for things to do. As you form your letters you may find that you begin to let your thoughts wander as your fingers produce the same form over and over again. Before long you'll find that you've filled full sheets of letters and that you've begun to master the art without having to give it a lot of thought or serious effort.

Learning calligraphy can be a wonderful way to enhance many areas of your life. Adding this little decorative touch to everything from home décor to table settings can allow you to deepen your satisfaction in any area. Start practicing your calligraphy and letter forms today to begin to enhance your words and their impact tomorrow.

"One Day Origami Mastery" by Ellen Warren

[Excerpt from the first 3 Chapters]

The Basics

Are you looking for a hobby that is fun and easy to learn? Are you wanting to learn how to make your own decorations? Or, are you simply looking for a way to relax? Origami can be the way to answer yes to all of these questions.

What is Origami?

Origami is the art of folding paper to create a work of art. The word comes from Japanese, *ori* means "folding" and *kami* means "paper". How simple is that? Origami is based on simple principles and simple foundational folds, when combined, that can create complicated structures. While the term origami comes from Japan, paper folding existed in China long before it did Japan. People have been practicing paper folding for around 2,000 years. Origami is an ancient practice that is still relevant today. Paper folding serves several different functions.

Uses for Origami

Origami has long been used to create decorations. You can make centerpieces for tables at a party. You can decorate gift packages with origami shapes. You can make a string of origami wedding dresses to decorate for a bridal shower. The uses for origami-based decorations are only limited by your imagination.

Another use for origami is education. Paper folding offers children so many valuable lessons. First of all, origami improves hand-eye coordination. It's excellent for developing fine motor skills, and this is why origami has been used in teaching students with disabilities. Secondly, origami teaches sequencing and following instructions. If you don't follow the instructions exactly, your paper sculpture won't turn out right. In addition to these lessons, origami also teaches you how to focus and gain a sharper attention to detail. If you don't focus on what you're doing, the duck you're trying to make might end up looking like a dragon. Finally, origami teaches patience. You can't rush through the steps and expect a beautiful creation. You have to take your time when first learning a new shape. Even after you've mastered a shape, you still need to take your time because mistakes stand out in origami. Origami is a practice in beauty, and this can't be rushed.

Not only does origami serve decorative and educational purposes, but paper folding can be therapeutic, as well. The amount of focus that is required to successfully turn a piece of paper into a crane helps you take your mind off of your troubles. The patience needed to make intricate folds helps you relax. Overall, practicing origami has a calming effect.

If these reasons weren't enough to convince you to try origami, then the greatest reason of all will: it's fun! Origami was practiced by the Imperial Court of Japan over 1,000 years ago as a way of passing the time, and it's still used the same way today. You can create origami shapes while sitting at home. You can practice origami while waiting for a meeting to start (I might suggest that, while origami can help you make it through a boring meeting, you might not want to make a giraffe during a meeting and upset your boss!).

Simply origami is a great hobby to learn. You get all of these great benefits, and at little cost. With origami, you're not going to have the costs of other hobbies such as model airplane building. This is because the materials you need to create artistic shapes out of paper are minimal.

What You Need for Origami

The basic tools you use in origami are your hands. That's what makes origami great. You don't have to buy specific tools for the hobby. There's no glue or paint to buy. You don't have to use special cutting tools. Instead, you use the basic tools you were born with: your hands.

Other than your hands, you need paper. That's it. Origami is nothing more than folding paper with your hands in a series of steps to create a shape. The cost of origami is much cheaper than scrapbooking. You're not going to run into the same costs with origami as you would collecting stamps or coins because paper is highly available and relatively cheap (unless you want a specific design, but even then it's still not costly). You can buy a 500 count package of origami paper that contains multiple colors for under $20. That's 500 paper sculptures for under $20.

Origami Paper

Kami, traditional origami paper, is thin so that it can be folded easily. It's also weighted enough to hold a crease, but not too heavy that you can't eliminate a crease if you make a mistake. It's usually colored on side and white on the other. *Kami* comes in many different sizes, but a common size that is sold is a 6 in. square.

In addition to *kami*, foil-backed paper can be used if you want to make a design that is intricate and requires the paper to hold its fold. Foil-backed paper is a thin sheet of aluminum foil that is glued to a thin sheet of paper. Some origami enthusiasts like using foil-backed paper to practice intricate fold patterns because of its ability to hold a crease well. This ability can also be a problem if using foil-backed paper at other times because it's unforgiving: once you a mistake, the mistake will show more than with other paper types.

You Could Use Other Tools If You Needed To

Origami is such a versatile hobby. If you don't have any *kami* near you, you can always use copy paper. You'd simply have to cut the 8 ½ in. x 11 in. copy paper into a square. You'd need a pair of scissors.

As for making different size sculptures, you can purchase different sizes of origami paper. Or, you can buy a larger size, say a 10 in. square and cut a piece down to the size you want. If you do this, you'll have more origami paper to use. Also, you don't have to just buy squares. Origami paper also comes in other shapes, like a circle, for sculptures that require such shapes. Again, you can always cut these shapes out of a square piece of paper. In these cases, you would need scissors, ruler, pair of compasses, and a pencil to mark where to cut.

Another tool that is used by some origami practitioners is a bone folder. A bone folder is used to mark and crease paper. Originally bone folders were made from animal bones, thus the name. Today, bone folders are made from plastic, as well.

Now that you know the basics of origami and you see how useful and efficient origami is as a hobby, you're probably itching to get your hands on a piece of paper and begin folding. Enthusiasm is good. It'll help you appreciate the art of origami more, and will make your origami experience more enjoyable. If you're ready to learn origami, the place to begin is with some standard fold techniques, but before you take these on it might be helpful to know some tips for great looking origami.

Some Tips <u>Before</u> You Begin

As you've seen already, origami can be a fun hobby to learn. Yet, origami is more than a hobby. It's an art form. Truthfully, it will take time to learn how to fold the paper properly to create beautiful paper sculptures. Anything creative takes effort, but the results can be astounding. If you want astounding origami figures, there are a few tips that can help you.

Take Your Time

Origami is a practice in patience. Don't rush through the folds. Take the time to make each fold correctly. If you don't take your time to correctly execute each step, your figure will not look right in the end. More than that, origami is supposed to be relaxing. You can't relax if you're rushing through the steps. If you want origami to stay enjoyable, take your time. Enjoy the process.

Go For Accuracy

More than being a practice in patience, origami is a practice in accuracy. Review the diagrams. Follow the instructions exactly as they are given. Make precision folds. Be sure that edges match up when folding. Be precise. The beauty of origami is sharp lines and symmetry. Lacking accuracy in your folding destroys this beauty. Start with soft creases. If you make a mistake, correcting the mistake will be easier with a soft crease. With a soft crease, the evidence of a mistake will not be as evident, if it's evident at all. Once you've made the fold and it's accurate, make the crease again using a hard crease.

Work in a Clean Area

This includes having clean hands before you start. You don't want dirty hands to ruin the paper. Also, if you're using a flat surface on which to fold, make sure it's clean, as well. Again, you don't want stains on your completed figure.

Learn as Much as You Can

Don't settle for knowing a few simple patterns. Increase your repertoire. Work your way through various levels of difficulty. Start with simple patterns and work up to difficult patterns. Read up on origami on the internet. Watch instructional videos. Experiment with the process. Create your own designs. Get the most out of origami. It's your hobby. More than that, it's your craft. It's your art form.

Practice

Origami, like any art that requires skill, needs to be practiced. The old saying, "practice makes perfect", holds true for origami. The more you practice folding, the better you will get at it. Practicing folding helps you to remember the steps. It also helps you remember the positions of the folds, as well. More than anything, by consistently folding, you'll reap all of the benefits of origami that were mentioned previously.

Don't Give Up

When you make a mistake, and you will, don't give up. Simply try again. You may be able to save the paper from a mistake, or you may have to use a new piece of paper. That's why you should always fold a new pattern on cheaper paper, in case you have to start over on a new piece of paper. You may want to attempt to patterns on copy paper, so that you won't waste *kami*. Also, you may want to work through a new design with a larger piece of paper. This will help you complete the folds completely. Once you mastered the new design, you can then move to a smaller, more expensive piece of paper.

Show Off Your Paper Sculptures

Find some way to exhibit your creations. Take a picture of them to share on social media. Keep a photo album. Display them somewhere in your house. Decorate your office with your origami sculptures. Use your origami artwork to decorate for special events. Give them away as gifts. Join an online origami forum where you can discuss origami and share your creations. Host an origami party where your friends can gather to origami together. Let others enjoy your newly learned talent.

Without Further Ado

Now that all of the basics of origami have been discussed, it's time to get down to the nitty-gritty. The following chapters will take you through your first fold all the way to difficult patterns. By practicing the instructions provided in the remainder of this book, you'll have learned 10 origami designs. That's a strong beginning that you can build upon as you practice your new hobby.

[Excerpt from the first 3 Chapters]

www.ingramcontent.com/pod-product-compliance
Lightning Source LLC
Chambersburg PA
CBHW062111280526
45788CB00003B/1433